Fact Finders®

EXPLORING HISTORY THROUGH FOOD

COLONIAL COOKING

by Susan Dosier

CAPSTONE PRESS
a capstone imprint

Fact Finder Books are published by Capstone Press,
1710 Roe Crest Drive, North Mankato, Minnesota 56003.
www.mycapstone.com

Library of Congress Cataloging-in-Publication Data
Names: Dosier, Susan, author.
Title: Colonial cooking / by Susan Dosier.
Description: North Mankato, Minnesota: Capstone Press, [2017] |
Series: Fact finders. Exploring history through food | Audience: Ages 9–12. |
   Audience: Grades 4–6. | Includes bibliographical references and index.
Identifiers: LCCN 2015051232| ISBN 9781515723561 (library binding) |
   ISBN 9781515723608 (ebook pdf)
Subjects: LCSH: Cooking, American—History—Juvenile literature. | United
   States—History—Colonial period, ca. 1600-1775—Juvenile literature. |
   Food habits—United States—History—17th century—Juvenile literature. |
   Food habits—United States—History—18th century—Juvenile literature. | LCGFT: Cookbooks.
Classification: LCC TX715 .D68747 2017 | DDC 641.5973/09032—dc23
LC record available at http://lccn.loc.gov/2015051232

Editorial Credits
Editor: Nikki Potts
Designer: Kayla Rossow
Media Researcher: Jo Miller
Production Specialist: Steve Walker

Photo Credits
Capstone Studio: Karon Dubke, back cover (country captain and Indian pudding), 1 (country
captain), 13, 17; Corbis: AS400 DB, 6, Blend Images/John Block/RF, 1 (apple pie), 27; Newscom:
Oronoz/Album, 18; North Wind Picture Archives, cover (inset); Shutterstock: Africa Studio, 16,
cover (wheat and background), Amallia Eka, 1 (mashed pumpkin), 9, dani3315, 15, endeavor, 20, 22,
Fanfo, back cover (pepper pot), 29, Lorraine Kourafas, 1 (boiled dinner), 25, Sebastian Duda, 10

Design Elements
Shutterstock: 4Max, Amawasri Pakdara, Mliberra, Vitaly Korovin

Printed and bound in the USA
009670CGF16

TABLE OF CONTENTS

KITCHEN SAFETY

1. Make sure your hair and clothes will not be in the way while you are cooking.
2. Keep a fire extinguisher in the kitchen. Never put water on a grease fire.
3. Wash your hands with soap before you start to cook. Wash your hands with soap again after you handle meat or poultry.
4. Ask an adult for help with sharp knives, the stove, the oven, and all electrical appliances.
5. Turn handles of pots and pans to the middle of the stove. A person walking by could run into handles that stick out toward the room.
6. Use pot holders to take dishes out of the oven.
7. Wash all fruits and vegetables.
8. Always use a clean cutting board. Wash the cutting board thoroughly after cutting meat or poultry.
9. Wipe up spills immediately.
10. Store leftovers properly. Do not leave leftovers out at room temperature for more than two hours.

METRIC CONVERSION

U.S.	Canada	U.S.	Canada	Fahrenheit	Celsius
1 quart	1 liter	1/4 teaspoon	1 mL	325 degrees	160 degrees
1 ounce	30 grams	1/2 teaspoon	2 mL	350 degrees	180 degrees
2 ounces	55 grams	1 teaspoon	5 mL	375 degrees	190 degrees
4 ounces	85 gram	1 tablespoon	15 mL	400 degrees	200 degrees
1/2 pound	225 grams	1/4 cup	50 mL	425 degrees	220 degrees
1 pound	455 grams	1/3 cup	75 m		
		1/2 cup	125 mL		
		2/3 cup	150 mL		
		3/4 cup	175 mL		
		1 cup	250 mL		

COOKING EQUIPMENT

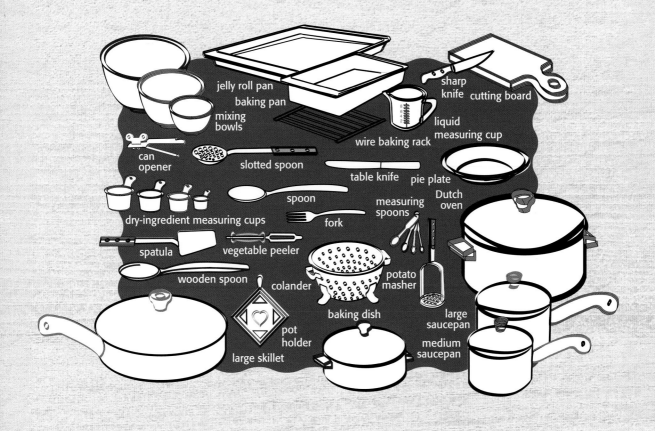

jelly roll pan

baking pan

mixing bowls

sharp knife

cutting board

can opener

slotted spoon

liquid measuring cup

wire baking rack

table knife

pie plate

dry-ingredient measuring cups

spoon

fork

measuring spoons

Dutch oven

spatula

vegetable peeler

wooden spoon

colander

potato masher

pot holder

baking dish

large saucepan

large skillet

medium saucepan

CHAPTER 1

THE PILGRIMS COME TO PLYMOUTH

In 1620 a religious group from England known as the **Pilgrims** anchored their ships off the coast of Massachusetts. They were the first Europeans to build a permanent settlement in this area of North America.

The Pilgrims founded the colony of Plymouth. About half of the colonists died of sickness or **starvation** during the first winter. Plymouth colony would not have survived without the help of a neighboring American Indian tribe, the Wampanoags.

In the spring Wampanoag tribe members showed the Pilgrims where to hunt and fish and how to plant crops. The Wampanoags wanted a peaceful friendship with the colonists. They also hoped the Europeans would protect them from other American Indian tribes.

New England Pilgrims and American Indians join for the first Thanksgiving.

American Indians celebrated harvest festivals of thanksgiving long before the Pilgrims. The American Indians prepared this feast and celebration to ask the Creator's blessings for the following year. They believed in a Creator who provided them with food from the earth.

In October of 1621 the Pilgrims and the Wampanoag tribe joined in a celebration. For three days everyone feasted and played games.

Today no one is certain what the colonists and Wampanoags ate at the first Thanksgiving meal. They probably stewed and roasted wild turkey, duck, or pigeon, and antelope or deer. Cooks may have served squash, pumpkin, sweet potatoes, corn pudding, and dried berries. They probably steamed lobster, cod, or sturgeon in layers of seaweed over hot coals.

Like the American Indians the colonists continued to celebrate Thanksgiving every year after harvesting their crops. By the mid-1600s Thanksgiving took place on a Thursday every fall in New England. Thanksgiving became a national holiday in 1863.

Pilgrim—a member of the religious group that separated from the Church of England and founded Plymouth, Massachusetts, in 1620
starvation—the condition of suffering or dying from lack of food

CHAPTER 2

THE NEW ENGLAND COLONIES

By the mid-1700s, 13 English colonies stretched along the eastern coast of North America. Differences in climate, soil, and the traditions of the settlers separated the colonies into three regions. The regions were the New England colonies, the middle colonies, and the southern colonies.

Most of the New England and southern colonists came from England. Early colonists survived on foods that grew wild in the region. They also depended on the animals they brought with them from England as a food source. Seeds brought over on their journey did not flourish in the rocky soil. Colonists called this soil hard scrabble.

The New England colonies had a short growing season and long, cold winters. During the winter New Englanders turned to fishing as a means of survival.

New Englanders learned to make breads, stews, puddings, and jams from native plants. These plants included corn, squash, sweet potatoes, pumpkins, and beans. Wild gooseberries, mulberries, and cranberries grew along the coast.

MASHED PUMPKIN

EQUIPMENT

paper towel or napkin
cutting board
sharp knife
large spoon
potato masher or fork

jelly roll pan, 13-inch by
8-inch (33-centimeter by
    20-cm)
fork
pot holders

large bowl
liquid measuring cup
measuring spoon

INGREDIENTS

1 tablespoon butter or
    margarine for greasing
1 small pumpkin
1/4 cup cider vinegar

1 teaspoon ginger
4 tablespoons
    (1/2 stick) butter

Ask an adult to help you prepare this recipe.

1. Preheat oven to 325°F (160°C). Use paper towel or
   napkin dabbed with 1 tablespoon butter or margarine to lightly grease pan.

2. Wash pumpkin. Ask an adult to cut it in half crosswise.

3. Use spoon to scoop out seeds. Discard seeds.

4. Place the pumpkin halves, cut-side down, on pan. Be sure to use a pan
   with sides because pumpkin juices may ooze out.

5. Bake pumpkin 45 minutes or until fork easily pierces the fleshy part.
   Cool 10 minutes.

6. Ask an adult to peel the skin off the pumpkin with a sharp knife.

7. Put pumpkin in bowl. Mash pumpkin with potato masher or fork.

8. Stir in 4 tablespoons butter, 1/4 cup vinegar, and 1 teaspoon ginger. Serve hot.

Makes 6 servings.

CHAPTER 3

THE MIDDLE AND SOUTHERN COLONIES

Many people who lived in the middle colonies came from western Europe. The middle colonies had a long growing season and rich soil. Colonists planted pea, pear, and apple seeds that they had carried over from Europe. The warm climate and rich soil supported wheat, rye, and other grains. This area of colonial America became known as the breadbasket.

Some southern colonists grew tobacco, rice, and **indigo** on **plantations**. Slaves from West Africa taught southern colonists how to grow rice. Rice became a major export of North Carolina and South Carolina. Southern colonists also planted large orchards of apple, pear, cherry, peach, and plum trees. Grapes, raspberries, and strawberries grew wild.

indigo—a crop grown on plantations for trade purposes; indigo plants have dark purple berries that can be made into a dye

plantation—large farm found in warm areas; before the Civil War, plantations in the South used slave labor

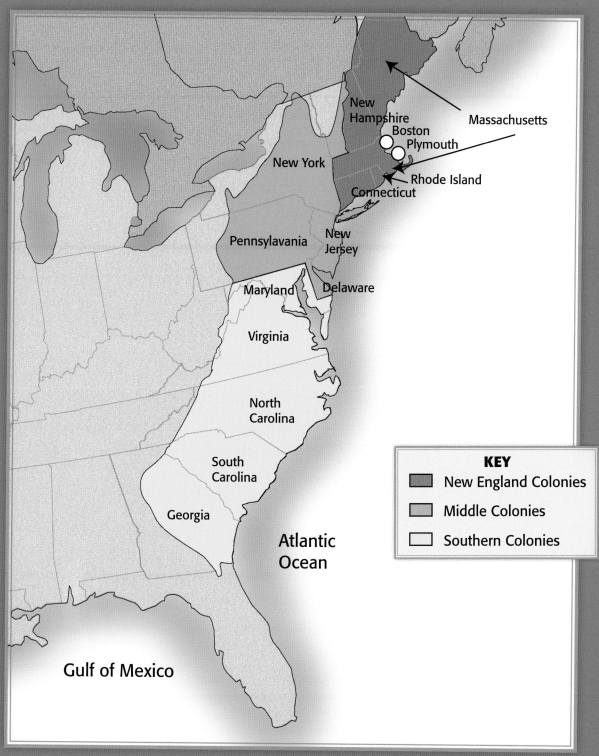

New Hampshire

New York

Boston

Plymouth

Massachusetts

Rhode Island

Connecticut

Pennsylavania

New Jersey

Maryland

Delaware

Virginia

North Carolina

South Carolina

Georgia

Atlantic Ocean

Gulf of Mexico

KEY

New England Colonies

Middle Colonies

Southern Colonies

COUNTRY CAPTAIN

Country Captain is a southern colonial rice dish. This recipe probably received its name from sea captains or trading ships.

INGREDIENTS

3 slices bacon

4 boneless chicken breast halves

1 medium onion

1 green bell pepper

1 (28-ounce) can diced tomatoes, undrained

1/3 cup raisins

1 tablespoon brown sugar

2 teaspoons curry powder

1/2 teaspoon dried thyme

2 cups water

1 teaspoon salt

2 cups instant rice

1/3 cup slivered almonds

EQUIPMENT

Dutch oven or large saucepan

tongs

paper towel

spatula

cutting board

sharp knife

wooden spoon

can opener

dry-ingredient measuring cups

measuring spoons

liquid measuring cup

medium saucepan

Ask an adult to help you prepare this recipe.

1. Cook three slices of bacon in Dutch oven or saucepan until crispy. Remove bacon to paper towel and set aside. Leave bacon drippings in Dutch oven.

2. Cook chicken breasts in Dutch oven or saucepan over medium heat.
   Brown both sides.

3. Place chicken on cutting board. Cut into bite-sized chunks.

4. Remove skin from onion. Chop onion.

5. Remove seeds from bell pepper. Chop bell pepper.

6. Cook onion and bell pepper in Dutch oven 3 minutes, stirring occasionally.

7. Add 1 (28-ounce) can tomatoes, 1/3 cup raisins, 1 tablespoon brown sugar,
   2 teaspoons curry powder, and 1/2 teaspoon thyme.

8. Add chicken pieces to tomato mixture. Stir well. Bring to boil.
   Reduce heat to low. Cook uncovered, 20 minutes.

9. Put 2 cups water and 1 teaspoon salt in the medium saucepan.
   Bring to a boil. Add 2 cups instant rice. Cover and remove from heat.
   Let stand for 5 minutes.

10. Place chicken mixture on the rice. Sprinkle with almonds before serving.

Makes 4 servings.

CHAPTER 4

CORN FOR MEALS AND MORE

The American Indians grew corn along the eastern coast of North America long before the English colonists arrived. American Indians depended on corn for their survival. They also honored corn in religious ceremonies and celebrations.

The colonists ate a dish made from corn at almost every meal. American Indians introduced the Pilgrims to corn on the cob, popcorn, and **hominy**.

The American Indians taught colonists how to grind corn into meal with a **mortar and pestle**. A mortar was a hollowed-out piece of wood or stone. Colonists dumped the corn into the mortar and pounded it with the hammer-like pestle. Cooks used cornmeal in breads, biscuits, pies, and puddings.

hominy—kernels of dried corn from which the hulls have been removed by soaking and boiling in water containing lye

mortar and pestle—hollowed-out piece of wood or stone that corn was put into and then pounded with a hammer-like pestle

CHILDREN'S CHORES

Colonial children helped their parents gather and prepare food. They started doing chores at the age of 5 or 6. Children searched the forests for wild mushrooms, onions, mustard plants, dandelion greens, and celery. They picked nuts and wild fruit from bushes and trees.

In the evenings children sat by the fireplace and removed the kernels from ears of corn. They scraped the ears against a shovel blade to loosen the kernels. Colonial children also threaded fruits and vegetables on long strings. The strings were hung from the ceiling to dry. Colonists stored dried foods to eat later during winter.

corn being ground with a mortar and pestle

In colonial times pudding was similar to today's hot cereal. Colonists served pudding before the main course of a meal. Pudding sometimes was their entire meal. Colonists often invited guests to "Come for pudding time," which meant "Come in time for dinner."

Early colonists mixed cornmeal with water and sometimes a bit of molasses. They put the mixture in a cloth sack and then hung it over the fire for a few hours to boil. The mixture thickened as it cooked. Colonists sometimes made corn pudding by baking the ingredients in a pan. Cooks added ingredients such as milk and eggs to make the pudding richer. They also mixed in flour, salt, and sugar when they were available.

Colonists used corn for more than cooking and eating. They often paid their taxes with corn instead of money. In the early 1600s Massachusetts colonists used corn and beans to vote. A kernel of corn stood for a yes vote. A bean was a no vote.

INDIAN PUDDING

INGREDIENTS

1 tablespoon butter or
   margarine for greasing
2-1/2 cups milk
3/4 cup cornmeal
2 eggs
1/2 cup molasses
1/4 teaspoon salt

EQUIPMENT

paper towel or napkin
medium saucepan
small baking dish
liquid measuring cup
dry-ingredient
   measuring cups

large spoon
small bowl
fork
measuring spoons
pot holders

Ask an adult to help you prepare this recipe.

1. Preheat oven to 300°F (150°C). Use a
   paper towel or napkin dabbed with
   1 tablespoon butter or margarine to
   lightly grease baking dish.

2. In saucepan stir 2-1/2 cups milk and
   3/4 cup cornmeal over medium heat.
   Cook, stirring often, about 15 minutes,
   until thickened.

3. In bowl lightly stir 2 eggs with fork. Gradually add eggs
   to hot mixture, stirring constantly, until well blended.

4. Add 1/2 cup molasses and 1/4 teaspoon salt. Stir.

5. Remove from heat. Pour into baking dish.

6. Bake uncovered for 45 minutes. Serve warm.

Makes 8 servings.

CHAPTER 5

THE COLONIAL KITCHEN

In many colonial homes the kitchen was the center of daily life. Families cooked, ate, slept, and worked in the kitchen.

In early colonial times cooking pots hung from a wooden lug pole stretched across the inside of a fireplace. Colonists made lug poles from green wood. When the wood dried, the lug pole was in danger of catching fire. Colonists replaced wooden lug poles often.

In the 1700s many colonists replaced the wooden lug pole with an iron lug pole. Many were connected to a hinge allowing the pole to be moved in and out of the fire.

Colonists fried foods in iron **spiders**. The large skillets had three short legs and a long handle, allowing the colonists to move the pan in and out of the fire.

spider—an iron skillet with three legs

A brick fireplace often took up an entire wall in the colonial kitchen. The kitchen fireplace was the only source of light and heat in some homes.

Colonial women set aside one day each week to bake bread. They made enough bread to last for an entire week. As towns grew bakeries became common. Colonists purchased various breads and biscuits from bakery shops.

The colonists made their own yeast for wheat and rye breads. Yeast bread bakes light and fluffy. To make yeast colonists let some dough age or sour. A small amount of sourdough was added to each loaf to make the bread rise.

Most early colonists baked their bread with cornmeal. Cornbread does not rise with yeast because the dough is thin and grainy. Early colonists kept trying to make a cornbread that would cook up light and fluffy like wheat bread. But the cornbread baked into a heavy, flat cake.

Beans were another very important food. Beans provided protein and took the place of meat in many dishes. Colonists dried large amounts of beans and stored them to use in winter. Pinto, lima, snap, kidney, wax, and pea beans grew well in New England colonies.

BOSTON BROWN BREAD

EQUIPMENT

paper towel or napkin
2 empty cans, 1-pound each
large mixing bowl
dry-ingredient measuring cups
measuring spoons
wooden spoon
medium mixing bowl
liquid measuring cup
aluminum foil
2 Dutch ovens with lids or
    2 large saucepans
2 thick dishtowels
toothpick
pot holders
wire baking rack
serrated knife

INGREDIENTS

2 tablespoons butter for greasing,
    separated into 1 tablespoon pieces
1 cup yellow cornmeal
1 cup rye flour
1 cup whole wheat flour
1 cup raisins
2 teaspoons baking soda
1 teaspoon salt
2 cups buttermilk
3/4 cup molasses

Ask an adult to help you prepare this recipe.

1. Use a paper towel or napkin dabbed with 1 tablespoon butter to thoroughly grease one empty can. Repeat step for the second empty can.
2. Stir together 1 cup cornmeal, 1 cup rye flour, 1 cup whole wheat flour, 1 cup raisins, 2 teaspoons baking soda, and 1 teaspoon salt in large mixing bowl.
3. In another bowl stir together 2 cups buttermilk and 3/4 cup molasses.
4. Add wet mixture to dry ingredients. Stir well.
5. Pour combined mixture into cans.
6. Cover each can tightly with aluminum foil.
7. Fold dish towels. Place one towel in bottom of each Dutch oven.
8. Place cans on folded towels.
9. Pour hot tap water into each Dutch oven or saucepan until it reaches halfway up the sides of empty cans. Place lids on Dutch ovens. (Ask and adult to help you with this step.)
10. Bring water to a boil. Reduce heat to medium-low. Boil gently 4 hours. Insert toothpick in center. If the toothpick comes out clean, the bread is done.
11. Using pot holders transfer cans to wire baking rack. (Ask and adult to help you with this step.)
12. Remove aluminum foil. Let stand 20 minutes. Gently remove bread from cans. Cool completely. Cut with serrated knife. (Ask an adult to help you with this step.)

Makes 2 small loaves.

BOSTON BAKED BEANS

The colonial town of Boston, Massachusetts, became known for baked beans. A religious group from England called the **Puritans** founded Boston. Sunday was a day of rest and prayer for the Puritans. They baked beans on Saturday night to eat on Sunday, their day of rest.

INGREDIENTS

1 pound dried navy (pea) beans
8 slices bacon
12 cups water
1 tablespoon butter or
    margarine for greasing
1 medium onion
3/4 cup molasses
1 teaspoon dry powdered mustard
1-1/2 teaspoons salt
1/2 teaspoon pepper

EQUIPMENT

colander
Dutch oven or
    large saucepan with lid
cutting board
sharp knife
liquid measuring cup
paper towel or napkin
slotted spoon
liquid measuring cup
measuring spoons
wooden spoon
pot holders
cake pan, 9-inches by 13-inches
    (23-cm by 33-cm)

Ask an adult to help you prepare this recipe.

1. Put 1 pound of beans in colander and rinse. Discard any split or dark beans. Pour beans in Dutch oven or saucepan.

2. Cut 8 slices of bacon into 1-inch (2.5-cm) pieces. Add bacon to beans.

3. Pour 12 cups water over beans. Bring to a boil over high heat.

4. Reduce heat to medium-low. Cover and cook gently 1-1/2 hours or until beans are tender.

5. Preheat oven to 350°F (180°C). Use paper towel or napkin dabbed with 1 tablespoon butter or margarine to lightly grease baking dish.

6. Remove beans from Dutch oven with slotted spoon. Add beans to cake pan. Save bean-cooking liquid.

7. Peel skin from onion. Chop onion. (Ask an adult to help you with this step.)

8. Add chopped onion, 3/4 cup molasses, 1 teaspoon dry powdered mustard, 1-1/2 teaspoons salt, and 1/2 teaspoon pepper to beans. Pour in 1-1/2 cups of bean cooking liquid. Stir well.

9. Bake uncovered for 45 minutes. Let cool and serve.

Puritan—a member of the religious group that wanted to purify the Church of England; the Puritans founded Boston, Massachusetts, in 1630.

CHAPTER 6

MEATS OF NORTH AMERICA

In the warmer months colonists and American Indians hunted deer, moose, elk, rabbits, and squirrels. During the winter many of these animals migrated to warmer climates. American Indians were familiar with the migrating habits of the animals. They often moved with the animals.

American Indians and colonists also hunted birds. Geese, **partridges**, ducks, pigeons, and turkeys were plentiful in the summer and autumn.

The colonists fished the coastal waters and rivers. They caught cod, mackerel, sturgeon, lobsters, and crabs. Many colonists dug for oysters and clams on eastern beaches. New England colonists relied on seafood when other animals migrated.

Colonists brought farm animals from Europe. Many cows, pigs, horses, and chickens survived the journey. Many colonists ate pork, ham, and bacon.

The colonists preserved some meat to eat during winter. To preserve meat the colonists salted, smoked, and dried it. Colonial cooks often boiled, stewed, or roasted their meats.

partridge—a plump game bird that has gray, brown, and white feathers

NEW ENGLAND BOILED DINNER

INGREDIENTS

3 to 4 pounds corned beef
6 cups water
6 large carrots
8 potatoes, unpeeled
2 cups water
1 small head cabbage
7 cups water

EQUIPMENT

Dutch oven or large
   saucepan with lid
liquid measuring cup
vegetable peeler
sharp knife
cutting board

Ask an adult to help you prepare this recipe.

1. Rinse beef in cold water. Place beef in Dutch oven or saucepan. Add 6 cups water.

2. Bring to boil over high heat. Reduce heat to medium. Cover and cook 1 hour.

3. Peel carrots. Cut 6 carrots into 1-inch (2.5-cm) pieces. (Ask an adult to help you with this step.)

4. Add carrot pieces, potatoes, and 2 cups water to beef. Cover and cook 30 minutes.

5. Cut cabbage into quarters. Add cabbage and 7 cups water to beef. (Ask an adult to help you with this step.)

6. Cover and cook 15 minutes.

Makes 6 servings.

CHAPTER 7

SWEET TREATS

Dessert ingredients, such as butter, eggs, and sugar, were expensive and limited. Most colonists could not afford much sugar and considered it a treasured possession. Brown sugar was less expensive and was often used instead of white sugar. Many saved desserts for special occasions.

Most colonial desserts contained fruit. Some fruits grew wild. Others grew from seeds brought from Europe. Colonists picked grapes, apples, plums, strawberries, raspberries, and blackberries to bake into pies.

When they lacked ingredients, colonists invented desserts. Colonial cooks mixed fruit with cornmeal dumplings and made desserts called slumps and grunts. Colonists sometimes rolled the fruit in a layer of dough for cobblers and **pandowdies**. The desserts were sweetened with sugar, molasses, maple syrup, or honey.

pandowdy—a deep-dish spiced apple dessert sweetened with sugar, molasses, or maple syrup and covered with a rich crust

APPLE PIE

INGREDIENTS

2 refrigerated pie crusts

1 tablespoon butter

5 to 6 Granny Smith or other
   tart baking apples, unpeeled

1/4 cup maple syrup or molasses

1/2 teaspoon cinnamon

2 tablespoons butter

EQUIPMENT

9-inch (23-cm)
   pie plate

paper towel or napkin

cutting board

sharp knife

liquid measuring cup

measuring spoons

table knife

fork

pot holders

Ask an adult to help you prepare this recipe.

1. Let pie crusts stand at room temperature
   for 15 minutes.

2. Preheat oven to 375°F (190°C). Use a paper
   towel or napkin dabbed with 1 tablespoon
   butter to lightly grease pie plate. Place bottom crust in pie plate.

3. Wash apples. Cut each apple into 8 wedges. Cut out seeds and cores.
   Place apples in pie plate. (Ask an adult to help you with this step.)

4. Drizzle 1/4 cup maple syrup on top and sprinkle 1/2 teaspoon cinnamon over apples.

5. Cut 2 tablespoons butter into little pieces. Dot the tops of apples with butter.
   (Ask an adult to help you with this step.)

6. Turn second pie crust upside down over apples. Trim off extra pastry along edges.
   Fold edges under bottom crust. Press around edges with fork tines.

7. Cut 4 1-inch (2.5-cm) angled slits near center of crust for steam to escape.
   (Ask an adult to help you with this step.)

8. Bake 30 to 35 minutes.

Makes 8 servings.

27

THE REVOLUTIONARY WAR

The colonies were under British rule. They began putting taxes on food and other goods brought into the colonies. Colonists thought this was unfair. The laws and taxes pushed the colonists to consider creating a country of their own.

The British king, George III, did not want to give up the colonies in North America. He sent an army of soldiers to North America to enforce British rule. This led to the Revolutionary War (1775-1783). Colonists formed an American army to battle the English soldiers.

Many colonial soldiers bought food from farmers or nearby towns during the Revolutionary War. The British soldiers' food came from England on supply ships.

Both British and colonial soldiers often went hungry during the Revolutionary War. The soldiers foraged for many of their meals.

In 1781 the British surrendered at Yorktown. The colonists gained their independence. The leaders of the 13 colonies named their new country the United States of America.

PHILADELPHIA PEPPER POT

INGREDIENTS

1 pound mild beef or pork sausage
1 large onion
2 celery stalks
2 green peppers
3 large potatoes, unpeeled
1 teaspoon dried parsley
5 cups water
1 teaspoon ground pepper
1/2 teaspoon ground cloves

EQUIPMENT

Dutch oven or large skillet with lid
spatula
cutting board
sharp knife
liquid measuring cup
measuring spoons

Ask an adult to help you prepare
this recipe.

1. Brown sausage in Dutch oven or
   skillet over medium high heat.
2. Break up sausage with spatula.
3. Peel skin from onion. Chop onion.
4. Chop celery into 1/4-inch
   (0.6-cm) slices.
5. Remove seeds from bell peppers. Chop bell peppers.
6. Cut potatoes into 1/2-inch (1.3-cm) slices. Cut slices into bite-sized chunks.
7. Add onion, celery, bell peppers, potatoes, and parsley to Dutch oven.
8. Add 5 cups water.
9. Add 1 teaspoon pepper and 1/2 teaspoon cloves.
10. Bring soup to boil over high heat. Reduce heat to medium. Cover and cook 1 hour.

Makes 6 servings.

GLOSSARY

Dutch oven (DUHCH-UHV-uhn)—a large covered pot

forage (FOR-ij)—to search for food in a surrounding area

hominy (HOHM-i-nee)—kernels of dried corn from which the hulls have been removed by soaking and boiling in water containing lye

indigo (IN-duh-goh)—a crop grown on plantations for trade purposes; indigo plants have dark purple berries that can be made into a dye

mortar and pestle (MOR-tur-PES-tuhl)—hollowed-out piece of wood or stone that corn was put into and then pounded with a hammer-like pestle

pandowdy—a deep-dish spiced apple dessert sweetened with sugar, molasses, or maple syrup and covered with a rich crust

partridge (PAR-trij)—a plump game bird that has gray, brown, and white feathers

Pilgrim (PIL-gruhm)—a member of the religious group that separated from the Church of England and founded Plymouth, Massachusetts, in 1620

plantation (plan-TAY-shuhn)—large farm found in warm areas; before the Civil War, plantations in the South used slave labor

porridge (POR-ij)—a breakfast food made by boiling oats or other grains in milk or water until the mixture is thick

Puritan (PYUR-uht-un)—a member of the religious group that wanted to purify the Church of England; the Puritans founded Boston, Massachusetts, in 1630.

spider (SPYE-dur)—an iron skillet with three legs

starvation (star-VAY-shuhn)—the condition of suffering or dying from lack of food

READ MORE

Fajardo, Anika. *The Dish on Food and Farming in Colonial America.* Life in the American Colonies. North Mankato, Minn.: Capstone Press, 2012.

Raum, Elizabeth. *The Scoop on Clothes, Homes, and Daily Life in Colonial America.* Life in the American Colonies. North Mankato, Minn.: Capstone Press, 2011.

Samuels, Charlie. *A Timeline of the Colonial World. History Highlights.* New York: Gareth Stevens Pub., 2010.

INTERNET SITES

FactHound offers a safe, fun way to find Internet sites related to this book. All of the sites on FactHound have been researched by our staff.

Here's all you do:

Visit *www.facthound.com*

Type in this code: 9781515723561

Super-cool stuff! Check out projects, games and lots more at www.capstonekids.com

INDEX